DEVOTION

To Nan,

with very best wishes,

Laurens San?

at Totnigh
12 May 1980

BY THE SAME AUTHOR

Opposite Views
The Drowned River
The Kingdom of Atlas

LAWRENCE SAIL

Devotions

SECKER & WARBURG
LONDON

First published in England 1987 by
Martin Secker & Warburg Limited
54 Poland Street, London W1V 3DF

Reprinted 1987

Copyright © Lawrence Sail 1987

British Library Cataloguing in Publication Data

Sail, Lawrence
Devotions.
I. Title
821'.914   PR6069.A418

ISBN 0-436-44081-4

ACKNOWLEDGEMENTS

Argo, Encounter, Oxford Magazine, Poetry Nation Review, Poetry Review, Prospice, Resurgence, Words, Schools Poetry Society, Enitharmon Press, The Mandeville Press, Harry Chambers/Peterloo Poets, Little, Brown & Co. (Boston/Toronto), Macmillan (London).

A number of the poems have been broadcast on *Poetry Now*, Radio 3. 'Snooker Players' was one of the winning poems in the 'Video Poetry' project organised jointly by Television South West and South West Arts.

Typeset by Inforum Ltd, Portsmouth
Printed in England by
Redwood Burn Ltd, Trowbridge

CONTENTS

Snooker Players	1
Allotments	2
Tower Falling	3
Riverine	5
At Possenhofen	6
Reichert's Leap	7
Boatman Shot	8
Panopticon	10
Mineral Line	11
African Moments	13
Remembering Innsbruck	14
Goodbyes	16
Runners, Fading	17
Dreaming of my Father	18
A Tooth	19
Ring	20
Shots in the Dark	21
An Incident in Kent	22
Fable	24
Hallowe'en Lantern	25
Rain on Roses	26
For F.	27
Diastole, Systole	28
Rocamadour	29
Apples at Sunset	30
Remember	31
The Quarry at Haytor	32
Dufy Looks Out to Sea	33
English Versions	34
Cricket Scoreboard	35
Boxers	36
Executives Jogging	38

Two Figures	39
A Birthday Portrait	40
A Compliment to Pissarro	41
Nude Coming Downstairs	42
Mr and Mrs Campbell	43
The Cemetery at Gufidaun	44
Four Poems for Christmas	45
At Easter	47
The Lady Chapel, Long Melford	48
Shrine	50
Detail from 'St Nicholas Rebuking the Tempest'	51
Apologia	53
After the Whales	54
Off Weymouth	55
Audenade	56
Rower	57
The Poet who Hated Abroad	58
The Escaped Names	59
At Wyompont	60
The Dart Estuary: Whitsunday	62
The Artist at 81	63

To my friends

SNOOKER PLAYERS

They whistle the fine smoke
Of blue dust from the cue,
Suave as gunslingers, never
Twitching one muscle too few.
At ease, holstering their thumbs
In trimmest waistcoats, they await
Their opponent's slip, the easiest
Of shots miscalculated.
Their sleek heads shine, spangled
With the sure knowledge of every angle.

Once at the table, they bend
In level reverence, to squint
At globe after globe, each
With its window of light glinting
On cushioned greener-than-green,
The rounded image of reason.
One click and cosmology thrives,
All colours know their seasons
And tenderly God in white gloves
Retrieves each fallen planet with love.

Watching them, who could believe
In the world's lack of balance?
Tucked in this pocket of light
Everything seems to make sense –
Where grace is an endless break
And justice, skill repaid,
And all eclipses are merely
A heavenly snooker displayed.
Yet all around, in the framing
Darkness, doubt dogs the game.

ALLOTMENTS

for Charles Causley

Since time continues to demand its bleak honours,
let them be awarded here, where thrift cuts wastage
to a minimum – old elixirs corked with rag
in sheds as close and devotional as chantries –
where each new year the gaudy seed-packets signal
the resurrection of hope, and by grass duckboards
the twine unwinds to love in its fruiting season.

The allotments have become their own aerial view –
the land as it appears in the gunner's reticle,
squared into simple plots, as a god might see it,
familiar yet strange, the workings of creatures
who seem to believe, but almost as a hobby:
and always the same workings, set at the edges
of every railway journey and of dark canals.

Even the ornaments recur – the upturned bowls
riddled with couch-grass, or the bicycles leaning
at a post, or the smoke rising in unison
from autumn fires, or the clack of spades resounding,
or the soft shifting of sieves. Here time will run out
endlessly, but can never defeat the tenants
of the last real estate of common prayer.

TOWER FALLING

A plunging upper case T
gives *lumière* – history
unwritten in puffs of smoke
squirting like blank captions
from the base – only then, *son*,
the blunt bang of air
blocking the ears.

The tower is a pure gerund,
beyond recall, kneecapped,
a banana tree's pulp trunk
neatly panga-ed, but still
standing in the split second
when the tall house of cards
starts to go.

No one could really say
what is seen, or what
simply imagined – for instance,
all the pointing jarred
free, burnt on the retina
as a high grid limned in black
against the air;

or the whole brittle brick
rod becoming pliable
as hose, settling slightly
but staying there, in acute
focus at the street end,
for an instant, for ever, to sign
off with S.

Whole lifetimes wobble,
the child caught out lying
goes giddy and hot in the head,
Tolstoy writes *War and Peace*,
and the ship's funnel slides
downwards into the boiling
foam of dust.

The horizon advertises
a new absence. Later,
the vague beachcombers come
to hobble over the rubble,
eyes down – now and again
turning something with a foot,
then moving on.

RIVERINE

for Jim Reed

'. . . weil Glückseligkeit nicht ein Ideal der Vernunft, sondern
der Einbildung ist.'
Kant

Above the fall, of course, nothing is declined,
All gestures repeat an infinite concordance
In ranks of matching trees, each phase of moon,
The regular dimpling rain, whose liquid pebbles
Will always fall plumb dead centre, rippling out
And out in regular encores. Here, any number
Of silent kings might come and go, their beards
Miraculously still among rhythmic rowers;
Or ladies proffer or retrieve as many swords
As you like; or pale girls loosely wrapped in white
Drift smiling by, immersed in death's long dreaming.

Only at the lip, as the water silkily pours
And tips, does the river find time and tense, the lively
rage of moment, in which the unbottled torrent
Wells forward and down in plaited layer on layer
Of contradiction, wording into a love
Crazy with twists and turns and sudden pleas –
Too much always said, and always at too great length.
Yet what could be more reasonable than gravity?
And nothing dazzles more than the splinters thrown
Up from rocks, or shines more deeply than the coils
Of pools, or refreshes more from two meadows off.

Downstream, the estuary exhales, its broad banks
Smacking of salt. What were those distant chasms
Reeking of poet's garlic, those sleek distances
Higher than bluebell woods, except a long-ago
Love affair well within range of eloquence?
But the silver fish that thuds upstream risks even
The rosiest of its precious blood to haul
Its bursting muscle of self, that intent eye,
Back through the roaring foam to that calm notion
Where, unbroken, the waters of the womb still mull
All the unspoken possible words of happiness.

AT POSSENHOFEN

for John Mole

The meadow in its mildness stretches on
And on beside the waters of the lake
Whose shallows, cloudy as kaolin, support
Boat after boat saluting to the breeze.

Games are played, bright frisbees slice the air,
Children run about, fall and get up again.
Blue smoke drifts by from meat being burnt.
People are idly kissing and talking and jigging
Up and down by rubber dugouts, blowing
With their feet; or lying pegged out on little jetties
Which sacrifice them to the fiery summer sun.
Many also are swimming, close to some swans.

They have discovered an African freedom from scale,
Each has escaped to become a function of all –
All the brown bodies, the simple vanities
Of dark brown breasts and the swanky male bulge,
Or the strip of bikini swooping down between legs
To grip the minimal groin and shout, like that one
There, in fluorescent green, 'Look at my tan!' –
A whole species on holiday from hermeneutics!

As if history had no value but accretion,
Were really just a mad king or two building castles
In Spain or Bavaria, then quietly drowning,
Each in his own dark lake. But every garden
Of earthly delights will conjure the triumph of death:
Beyond the wood, the railway runs straight past
Bruegel's Spanish soldiery to soul's north,
That other nakedness, those other fires.

In today's breeze, boat after boat nods:
Beside the lake the meadow stretches on
South of Dachau. Here nobody sees more
Than what they see. No one mentions God.

REICHERT'S LEAP

Each hopeless stitch homemade – the futile skin
Out of which he would jump. It's too late now,
Even if he wanted, as surely he must be wanting,
To climb down. He crouches on the cold brow
Of madness, on the parapet's fine brink,
His breath smearing the air, an unused silence
Which might have been saving speech. *Here, what do you think?
I didn't mean it. Of course. It makes no sense.*
Or simply, *We'll have a drink and then I'll go
To embrace my poor wife and children. Later, we'll chat.*
Too late. They say the journalists wouldn't throw
Their story out of the window, and that was that.
He shifts like a bird – ridiculous, he fears.
Go on, you're chicken. He cannot, will not stay
For this. A puff of looping breath. The sheer
Drop. The stupid tower begins to sway
In his mind only. A final shuffle, and
A plop as into water. The deficient air
Fails to support him. A black duster lands,
Bundles into the ground. A brief affair.
Men in caps. Fuss. A canvas shroud.
A way elbowed through the encroaching crowd.

Which of us, from our tower, would not recall
This brute parabola of pride and fall? –
Late Romantics, fledgling birdmen all!

(*In December 1911 Walter Reichert, a self-employed tailor, attempted to fly from the Eiffel Tower.*)

BOATMAN SHOT

Reading it in the paper, it seemed quite simple –
The Times correspondent, coming to a lake
In northern El Salvador, had wanted to cross
With five other newsmen, in order to discover
Whether the army, American-trained, had killed
Some peasants in land the guerrillas controlled. Old story.

San Nicolas, the hamlet in the story,
Was just that, its people plain and simple –
As was the evidence that the army had killed
Possibly more than a hundred. Back on the lake
The boat sank, leaving the travellers to discover
Their own way home, with a day's jungle to cross.

Back in San Salvador, in the shadow of the cross,
The boatman tasted whisky, went the story,
For the first time ever, and was happy to discover
What kept the newsmen going. He found it simple –
Just as it had been to ferry them over the lake
And find the villagers whom the soldiers had killed.

Two days after, the National Guard, who killed
For a living, came and took the boatman to cross-
Examine him about the foreigners at the lake
And about his part in a bad news story
Implying abuse of human rights. It was simple –
The truth, they said, was all they wanted to discover.

Finally they released him, unable to discover
The truth of what had happened, or who had killed
The villagers. The boatman, back in his simple
House, began to realise that to cross
From one shore to another was a story
Which had its hidden depths, just like the lake.

Too late he glimpsed the figures rising from the lake,
Some dressed like soldiers, in green. They did not discover
Anything worth listening to in his story.
They took the boatman out of his house and killed
Him then and there. His widow bears the cross
Of seven children. The future looks very simple.

Suchitlan was the lake, Alas the boatman killed.
This poem is his, who discovered and ferried across
The necessary truth, keeping the story simple.

PANOPTICON

Fifty pop-up pictures, an index
Of where they travelled and with whom –
A Muscovite bell, the Alhambra, Baalbek,
The Reichenbach Falls and, time and again,
Mountains, glaciers, perilous bridges,
Subservient moraines.

One in five, in colour, shows
The family, skilfully arranged
In Monsieur Claudet's London studio –
Here is Nanny with the youngest boys
And here, Louisa, next to a mirror,
Posing with immodest poise.

How steadily they gaze, not minding
That somehow the ark has leaked a little,
Letting in an ironclad grinding
Somewhere off Cape Hellas – as well
As a bird's-eye view of a railway station
Clearly a target for shells.

One-handed, we can flick them through
Their circular tour at whirlwind speed –
Here they are again, still viewing
The nacreous *Sehenswürdigkeiten*
Of the 1850s: blandly aloof,
Quite impossible to frighten

But finally just too disconnected,
Too finely cut out in three dimensions.
Look at the distance between flat objects,
How each pebble glows and glows:
Between their eyes and ours that watch
The dead ground grows and grows.

MINERAL LINE

The first engine came
breasted with flags,
decked with flowers,
making brave smoke,
with a smiling mayor
riding the footplate!

It laid in its wake
railway curves,
chapels, pubs –
the classic way
to open up
a dark interior.

For a few years
the dark bright spar
came down the long ladder
propped against
the high hill,
to be sent to Wales:

For a few years
in open trucks
with wooden seats
passengers set at
forty-five degrees
were winched to heaven,

passing at mid-point
their mirror image,
the wailing car
of those already
judged and falling,
falling down.

Then, cheap ore
from Spain. The First
War. How soon
under the wheels
they bend and break,
they bend and break,
the syllables of dreams!

Someone still has
the station-master's
whistle, its throat
clogged green,
its silver slit
bearing teethmarks.

AFRICAN MOMENTS

1

What the sun most brightly shines on
is not the Presidential Suite
not the Hotel Continental
not the cinema's cool plush depths
not the taxidermist's trophies
not the straw of packing-cases
not the traffic lights and meters
not the haze of the loud bazaar
but on the puddle bright as tin
beneath the slum's one public tap
from which water slowly dripping
discharges all the wanton seeds
of hope which ride inside the belly
of every Trojan horse of a city.

2

Our host, apologetic, indicates
wood and canvas buckled on the verandah,
a torn rainbow of colours, with stiff limbs
wrecked at all angles – and, tight-lipped, explains,
'Damned hyenas, at the deck-chairs again.'

Later, when the boy has cleared the table,
he sighs a little, adding that he thinks
all history is really very simple.
Enter the tyrants, shouldering deck-chairs:
the people howl with laughter in their lairs.

REMEMBERING INNSBRUCK

for Catriona

Suddenly, there it was –
the entire city, unpacked
dazzling and undamaged,
sparking across the gap
of twenty-seven years
into the dull dark room,
as unpredictable
and vivid as the lightning
which highlights every detail
of a complicated tree.

For instance, the angle at which
the High Street statue wore
its halo rakishly forward,
the head about to be hoopla-ed –
as seen from the Café Schindler,
where the daily papers flapped
in bamboo holders gnarled
and yellow as old bone;
where cream swirled and blurred
into the strong black coffee.

And there were windowboxes
filled with crimson flowers;
the thick smell of lentils
in hallways of apartments;
gingerbread wrapped in the finest
transparent paper printed
with green and silver branches;
and to the north, the river,
an icy green-grey torrent
impervious to sunlight.

And I saw the toylike trams
with their open balconies and
leather bell-straps, rumbling
loudly over hollow bridges,
inveigling the peaceful outskirts;

and the cable-cars as they lifted,
swayed and fell through darkness;
and my sister of ten in tears
because it was all, she said,
too beautiful to look at.

Only then, in the shadows
of the everyday dark room
did I recognise just how
remembering is never
neutral, even when
cunningly it arrives
in Austrian disguise:
and once again I smelt burning –
the end of a world, the scent
of the crimson flowers of death.

GOODBYES

for Erica

From behind the door, a toe
waggled at knee height –
or an arm, or a head. As she goes
she comes back, or bits of her do,
like a party game which might
find room for mad Carew.

At ten she already seems
privy to the dark spell
of loss, the impossible dream
of love's impossible sorrows –
and can break it by saying farewells
over the head of tomorrow.

'Goodbye, goodbye – I've gone!'
Once more, the head. 'I'm still
here!' Her feet drum on
the stairs. Then, above,
a slowly receding drill –
the bodied echo of love.

RUNNERS, FADING

for Matthew

How long ago was it
when they broke from the line
at crazy speed, urged on
by the fear of not fitting
that first hedge-gap?

Before the race, waiting,
they had looked pitiful,
much too clumsy, their legs
too gawky, the black numbers
pinned on askew.

Standing, sucking their breath
and ignoring ahead,
they let their feet stutter
on wet grass. One or two tried
to tell a joke.

Then they were off, upping
and downing and jostling,
slowly spreading, starting
to move less up and down, more
smoothly along.

They have gone now, fading
into distance like a
new dimension, beyond
recognition: and we wait
as if for forgiveness.

Slumped, an obvious parent,
inside the steamed-up car,
I long to hear the plimp
of feet on tarmac: to see
you, returning.

DREAMING OF MY FATHER

Up and up together we went
Through the rich, narrow garden,
Me and my father. A steep ascent
And the stairs of grass were hard,
Filled in. He was leaving at last.
Ja, ja, die Treppe, he murmured,
Smiling, recalling the interred
Treads of the hollow past.

As we climbed, he began to reveal
The names of flowers: once he paused
To admire the progress of seeds sealed
In candy-stripe drinking-straws.
Twice, softly, he spoke my name –
But each time he did so, I heard
The voice of my stepmother – an absurd
Acoustic trick, I thought, or a game.

I looked at him, then realised:
This time *he* had lived longer.
Although he looked very tired, his eyes
Were just as blue as when, much younger,
He had ridden a donkey right through Crete,
His jacket loose about his shoulders,
Self-consciously handsome, and so bold
He had looked almost immune to defeat.

And now, gently, he was reciting
The names of all the plants that stood
In a warm hutch, the last on the right,
On a long shelf of wood.
They grew on dolls'-house teapots
Whose lids were turned upside down –
And every single one
Was a kind of forget-me-not.

A TOOTH

The bottom edges thin to a frill of bone,
Its top is a scrimshaw carved with a dream of home:
Inside, something secret – between dried bits of red,
A hollow D. And it gleams richly, like a stone
Enamelled by water washing over the riverbed.

How it calls for a socket, for a marching jaw,
For a full house snugly set! Yet is no talisman,
No white cliff waving its emblems to tearful exiles,
No headstone memory, not even a shallow store
For the fossil fragments of a lost childhood smile.

Only, once it was not: so that what it enfolds
Is a journey to death, but also a journey to life –
As if a single fleck of sperm had frozen
Solid and grown, right on the womb's threshold,
Prelude and aftermath equally blank, unchosen.

It is nothing more, though, than a flake of bone, a gap
Which will not last, the merest whistle in a word,
A single blob of rain lost in a lake,
Done without, discarded: and still it traps
The heart, demanding a status greater than keepsake.

I weigh it now in my hand – gingerly, lest
A jolt should send it rolling between the boards
Or into a dusty corner, to be lost for ever –
Shapeless as spilt milk, but for ever impressed
With the image of a daughter calmly asleep, who never

Wakes when someone slips a cold coin under
Her pillow, or complains about the taste
Of blood, old and metallic, infecting her dreams.
I try not to notice the time, or even to wonder
At how dark on the white bedlinen her fair head seems.

RING

As casually as passing the salt
You handed me your wedding ring to keep –
Such savour! Such half-witting balancing out!
And I was the star-struck native, exalted
Beyond reason by the curio, wondering how
It might have removed my soul in my sleep.

The names it bore had been inscribed
Fifty years before: years that have streamed
Wildly through its hoop and gone to air.
I think of its usage – the constant sliding
On and off, the warp of wear and tear,
A pledge less and less redeemed.

Through it, as lightly as a kiss
To a sleeping child, once the two of you blew
The South Sea Bubble of love's brief monsoon –
What I hold now is your shining vocative
Long since reduced to zero, the punched moon
Haunting the forest's dying avenues.

Perhaps if I held it up to my eye
I might see my father on a rare visit, bending
To kiss your hand: or putting it to my ear,
Would hear him laughing to the point of crying –
Or you saying, as you often do, *The war
Had a lot to do with the marriage ending.*

At my father's grave, the wind flicks
Through unkempt grass. You often stay up late
And wake early. And I am the star-struck native,
Unborn again, dazzled by a golden cervix,
Emblem of the gift that the two of you have given,
Worth every ounce of its weight.

SHOTS IN THE DARK

The pout of a single gun –
Like a clout, heard through
The smoke-puff of detonation,
A thick woollen sock of a sound
Aimed at the mind – which hares
Off, twitching at targets.

A second shot, a third –
A fourth. Soon we lose count,
Seeing only rabbits slewed
To a quick bloody halt, the birds
Crashing through moonlight, their wings
Breaking on earth's brittle boards.

Hours later, no respite:
St Julian madly cuts down
Creation. We see our own
Sprawled deaths, witness the murders,
Guiltily offer alibis,
Make helpful statements to the police.

Dawn – and the raging psychopath
Shrinks to one red barrel,
A blank machine set
In a field, to scare off crows.
Imagination, meanwhile,
Notches another bull's-eye.

AN INCIDENT IN KENT

for Elinor Moore

My daughter, at six, almost drowned
At a swimming pool in Kent, at a school.
It was nobody's fault – she had been in already,
Had dressed and returned and was bending down
To splash a friend who was still in the pool
When suddenly in she went, head

Over heels. As quickly the friend dived
To get her. That was all. Soon after,
She learned to swim. For her, what stays
Vivid is not the shock of revival,
But two boys and their unkind laughter
At seeing her baptised, buried and raised.

For me, what stays is what she said
At the time, hardly retrieved, gasping:
*I knew I was safe because I could see
The water, there, above my head.*
Words that might have been her last
Or locked in her throat for eternity –

And I think of Hugo at Soubise, sitting down
In a café with his mistress, ordering beer
And opening a paper without any foreboding
To read of his daughter's death by drowning –
*His face and his hair were wet with tears.
His poor hand was pressed to his heart as though . . .*

The rest of the story could hardly mean
More than post-mortem – the early mist,
The lightness of the dinghy, which made them ship
Two stones as ballast: Léopoldine
Changing her mind, unable to resist
Her husband's smile or the thought of the trip.

At Caudebec, yet more stones
To reassure cautious Maître Bazire,
The lawyer. Then, after a lull,

A sudden gust. All the weight thrown
To one side. Capsize. No help near.
Didine clinging for a time to the hull . . .

The mother sat, fingering strands
Of the drowned girl's hair, hour after hour.
She kept her red-checked dress to dote on,
Folded in a bag. With trembling hand,
I loved that poor child beyond my power
To express in words, the poet wrote.

What else could he write, but that the grass
Must grow, and children die – what do,
But volley the blanks of guilt and grief
At a God who had fallen to black farce?
What words, what art could see him through
To any believable kind of belief?

He could not help himself: each year
He wrote a poem for the rose-planted grave,
Phrase after phrase still keenly edged –
Till somehow he re-invented the world
Of love, by imagining being there: saved
By seeing the water above his head.

FABLE

He found a stone shaped like a heart
On a rattling beach, in the last spring
His parents shared. It needed no art,
Felt heavy, had good colouring,
Would pass for real, or once real, rather.
Smiling, he gave it to his father.

That summer she found a stone like a hand
In a stream, and on it painted a sleeve,
Black buttons, a white cuff and
One accusing finger leaving
No room for doubt, or little, rather.
She thought it would amuse her father.

Their father built a house of stones
Which, polished and angled, could skim the light
In rooms where now he lived alone.
Perhaps the children thought to write,
Perhaps he, with his hand on his heart,
Would swear he could feel the bleeding starting.

HALLOWE'EN LANTERN

In the darkness, a face, skull-nosed,
Saw-toothed, slit-eyed – each year
A child's wild one-man show
Of root savagery would glow
At the window, in a rough blur.

Its soft brain, very neatly
Gouged, spooned clean away,
Had left its crass top completely
Ill-fitting, a soup-pot where sweetly
The smell of burning stayed.

Crackling waxily, profane,
Neckless, a drunken dome,
It stood between curtain and pane
Facing the frost or the dark rain
Through which I shivered home.

My mind's a blank. What went on
Behind that grin, in those banging
Rooms which belong to no one?
My children will go, my wife has gone –
In the darkness I see a face, hanging.

RAIN ON ROSES

The house was sold four years ago, but still
It comes to haunt me, that soft image of rain,
Those oily, pudgy globules that would not spill
Down from the fine-toothed leaves, simply staying.
Shining with light, that knowledge which arrives
To drench the already drenched, those raindrops seemed
On guard, warding me off lest I should try
To penetrate the green leaves' shadowy dreams.

Were there, then, other secrets to be uncovered
By greater strength, by scattering what lay
Across the threshold – or was it just that love
Must sometimes guard its secrets to win the day?
I see those rosebuds kissing into air and throwing
The raindrops off, and still I do not know.

FOR F.

Here are the depths of the perfect tense,
At the hem of the sunlit fields,
Here are the dreaming shadows you sensed,
Where you and the world were a single presence
And love could always heal.

Here is the English Elsewhere repeated
In every exile's heart,
Where the lost summers of childhood, retreating
To musky darkness, are forever meeting
The lives that we still hope to start.

DIASTOLE, SYSTOLE

The heart is a window looking out
Onto a garden where all paths lead
Through past winters and future springs
Into the summer, drowning doubt
In hazy ease. Here, each seed
Fruits to the fullest bloom of being,
Knowing its end from the greenest start,
Aware that giving is a dying art.

The heart is a window looking in
Onto a room where all our past lives
Darken to sweet and painful shadows,
The time-locked womb where hope must begin
To recognise itself and thrive
If lover is ever to attain the rose –
The rose, my love, whose heart may yet distil
True fragrance, and leave the summer air fulfilled.

ROCAMADOUR

What light concealed, the darkness brings to light:
Seventy times seven, the human urges
Ranked in melting turrets, the wavering verges
Stacked in hope against the soul's dark night.

A fakir's bed of nails, on which to lay
An antidote to fear or to regret:
I wish, I wish – each tallow pronoun sweats
Its limited plea into the iron tray.

Across the walls, the proof, in solid stone,
A gallery of favours, faith rewarded:
Row after row of triumph, thanks recorded
To the Black Virgin – who sits upon her throne

With Jesus perched on the edge of her left knee.
Angular, rigid, candle-flames catching the lights
In her crown – and with eyes turned inward, blank as night,
Demanding everything, blind with certainty.

I lit a candle, too, and followed you out,
Hoping you had not seen. *Oh please, oh please* –
Clean as the mouth of a tunnel, that doorway cleaving
The darkness of faith and the pale day of doubt.

APPLES AT SUNSET

You doubt – but even today
In a squint angle of the house
I saw through to enough
Of orchard to be dazzled
By a sheer sheet of gold
Where row on cascading row
Of red apples blared –
A system so complete
To the core, that this one sudden
Segment of dying light
Lacked for nothing to be
Somehow more than itself.

But, because you doubt,
I can say nothing more than
I saw the apples at sunset –
And hope that you too may see
Beyond these fractions of words
To all that yet may be.
But *you* in this poem,
You protest, is me.

REMEMBER

Such acid, contradictory brightness
Of coldest red and fieriest green –

You look bewildered, almost frightened
By the sparks which sputter where light had been.

Late Roman candles choke in mud,
Vesuvius fizzles without conviction,

Catherine wheels jam or are dud,
Rockets sheer off into swift extinction:

And now not one, but two effigies go
Up in the flames which fitfully show

Your pale face, bravely still trying
To believe in colours wedded to a glow.

THE QUARRY AT HAYTOR

Each numb bud
held in a vice,
locked beyond echo
in its chamber of ice:

and the waterfall solid,
clipped to the sill
of the high scarp,
acutely still.

In the pent silence
we made birds sing,
shared the pulse
of water quickening:

and as we watched,
by our warm power
the soft-fleshed trees
burst into flower.

Later, autumn
rusted the heather
and the bright fern lay
like scattered feathers:

where the water fell
two lilies turned
and turned, forlorn
in a dark cistern.

Through the bullying wind
I heard you call,
faithful and fearful,
somehow appalled:

and looking back
I saw summer and spring,
the half-worked veins
still shining, shining.

DUFY LOOKS OUT TO SEA

You could call it Deauville, if it serves –
There may even be such a place –
But here is where the world ends,
The planet's last finical curve
Beyond the green pillar of port
And starboard's smart retort.

On the hunk of the pier's wooden hull
People, whittled down, turn back
From the brink again and again –
With hopeless bravado the gulls
Leave their shrill loops to subside
Between dripping stanchions and tide.

Offshore, all the world knows
What silence, what slow heave –
O Mort, vieux capitaine:
But look how the sky glows,
Brightest of blank blue slopes!
If it serves, you could call it hope.

ENGLISH VERSIONS

This is the English year's translation of sorrow –
A failed late May, in which tense families walk
Through dripping avenues of rhododendrons
Where rain has washed the flowers to mortal paleness.
Hearts ache by the dark, peaty lake, its surface
More wrinkled than a prune.

No horizon looks through into tomorrow,
But somewhere a smooth political voice keeps talking –
'Spend! Spend! Spend!' It bleakly booms, intent on
Drowning despair. In a flapping marquee, for sale,
Dogged home produce, damp books. A draw takes place
For remaindered June.

And here is the English calendar's rendering of bliss –
The uncut grass of wildly catholic meadows
Stained blue and red, beneath the massy heights
Of candled chestnuts: a sweetness of May air
That only lovers could hope to multiply
In naked heat.

Nothing conceivably could be added to this:
Faith is a static heat-haze, neither to nor fro,
Simple as the switchback lanes hemmed in so lightly
By cloudy drifts of cow-parsley. Overhead, somewhere,
June begins in a far calm lake of sky
Where sun and moon meet.

CRICKET SCOREBOARD

for Hubert Moore

History only begins
Outside, at the slits hacked
In the cereal packet, like a peepshow,
By a child on a wet day.
In their sharp morse the scorers
Claim every action for fact:
Yet here in the hutch's dark glow,
In the gloaming of grass-smell and resin,
All possible matches are played.

But for darkness and rain
Such heat would surely prove
Too rich, and the great sums set
In white, too bright a demonstration
Of time's endless curve. The canvas
On the warped rollers hardly moves:
By the loops of numbers boys sweat
The seasons away, yet remain
Fiercely devoted to their stations.

Meanwhile, out in the field
Whole careers go missing,
Fading in the breeze to a hum
Of bar-time conversations.
Team after team shakes down
To almanach averages – but this
Stays fresh through countless summers:
The sweet-smelling box which shields
Dark and triumphant declarations.

BOXERS

Between these twanging staves
Is only the bell's one-two –
Clock, Farewell or Surprise,
The crowd's cheers or boos.

Above the glossy shorts
They've only the silk of sweat,
And the blank grin that tries
To camouflage pain and regret.

They must keep dancing, keep
Those kidneys, cherry-red,
On the attack, or begging
Close into the head.

They must keep dancing, must
Avoid those double figures –
But such directness, in time,
Will take its toll of vigour:

Like passionate lovers they
Will tangle in the end,
And gently be eased apart
By their natty mutual friend.

Yet they allow those men
In the corners to give them stick
Till they wince, to sponge them, send them
Back to face the music.

Long before it's over
They want an end to harm,
To fall, *ponderoso*,
Into each other's arms.

But blood is blood, and besides
They can hear through the smoky din
That voice which is always waiting
On the far side of any win:

You're only just as good, son,
As you are in your next bout –
Darkness and common time,
And the bell ringing down and out.

EXECUTIVES JOGGING

They breast the mists
of the high pathways
at the city limits
early each Sunday,

clothing and conduct
both immaculate,
fists plugging air,
feet never sidetracked.

Worship for them
is to train the cells
to work for each other
in an anthem of angels –

yet, huffing and hugging
themselves, in time
they might be tripped up
by the smugness which primes

a Puritan ethic,
pumping their blood
through soft arteries
like a graph of good.

They turn coolly
down drives, limbs loose,
to a scant communion
of ryebread and juice

and are gone. Too early
to know if such pride
will appease the gods
or provoke them to homicide.

TWO FIGURES

Dart is deaf and digs the garden strip:
He wears blue trousers with a slick city stripe.
With them manacled to his legs he reaches the house
On a clicking bicycle heavy as any horse.
He wields the pump as if he wants to knock
The stuffing out of you. He also may take knick-knacks
That take his eye. Sometimes he asks to be fired.
Once he hurled a brick at our hired black Ford.
He talks to himself and seems to be quite at home.
His wife, seen once, is somehow part of him –
In curlers, with funny eyes and very short,
And a floral apron over a man's shirt.

And Membury the dwarf who lives just short
Of the thundering trains which every so often shoot
Smoke from the cutting up in a ragged fan –
Membury yellow as the *Beanos* and *Radio Funs*
In his front window, who really wears gaiters and hoards
All his money in a large tin box which he hides.
His darkened parlour smells in equal doses of cats,
Newsprint and pee. Not even *Comic Cuts*
Has anyone to beat him. His piping voice,
Absurdly shrill, seems caught in some mad vice:
He tries and tries to clear his little throat,
Nervous as a lizard, as if afraid of threats.

Both long dead – but here they come, unhurried,
The dark grotesques of vivid childhood fears,
Spotless in detail, arcing over the years,
Harbingers of all not dead, just buried.

A BIRTHDAY PORTRAIT

If I were painting you, I would ask you to sit
Here, against the trunk of the large horse chestnut –
In May, of course, with the vivid fan of green,
Ribbed and vaulted, enormously flicked open
In peacock display, the brightest royal flush
Of spring's matchless suit.

At your back, inviolable strength,
Ancient authority sucked once more into shadow –
Here all systems seem inward, each tongue of leaf
Has a trunk and branches, each single tree
Builds its own fleshy forests of pink and white
Rising in soft pagodas.

Underfoot, the ground is wormed by roots,
The delved earth sifted to a powder finer
Than hourglass grains. Overhead, long weathers
Express themselves in shifting syncopations
Of sound and silence, the sun's dark humming heat,
The moon's pale knowledge.

I would have only to watch you, as you sat
At the still hub, as you watched the fields turn,
The landscape make loving sense, even though you know
That hope is always deciduous, and hearts
Not always trumps . . . When you began to smile,
Then I would start to paint.

A COMPLIMENT TO PISSARRO

I have never been to Eragny and yet
It always seems to advance, slanting slightly,
To meet or greet me, spreading the long shadows
Of its trees and buildings across the evening sunlight.

I know its church, that spire's fine secret point
Escaping from ambushing trees. And those cows in the field –
If I had to, I could call all four by their names,
Just as I could the locals. Ask Mathilde.

I know which shutters creak, and how the barn
Must baffle the wind and harbour the hot hay;
And what the drenching moonlight might discover
Deep in the silent houses, where every day

Drifts to the grainy air of summer dusk
And the easy hours of two lying close, the lace
Curtain barely lifting to purple sky . . .
Of the artist and his easel, not a trace.

NUDE COMING DOWNSTAIRS

after Duchamp

I am not this one or that one,
here or now, then or when –
I am a multiple negative,
Never cancelling myself,
Not going upstairs.

I am not anything as simple
As the central figure: I've tried.
Even my sex is unclear,
I am so clad in movement,
So decently blurred.

For all I know, we might have
Stepped clean off the roundabout
Somewhere between *maybe*
And *has-been*, but forgetting nothing,
Expecting everything still.

One of us has to decide
What to do when we reach
The hall: how best to greet
Anyone who might be waiting
With flowers for me, for me.

MR AND MRS CAMPBELL

for Jimmy and Margie

For nineteen years, two continents and five countries
Your houses have been for me a style as concise
    As well-packed cases, a shorthand plural
    For what you value most.

I agree that in part it's a matter of pretty *objets* –
The stones you polish and, even though you possess
    Any number, can proudly name; or the silver
    From Ethiopia, or the rugs –

But emblems too: in an earlier age you might have
Been given the credit for first bringing marrows to Rome,
    Or sunflowers to Kenya, or both to Belgium.
    Nor should the world forget

The encouragement given such plants in quite other places,
Like Oundle and Kent. And besides, wherever you've lived,
    Paper globes have always flourished – and
    Light and lightness of touch.

Yet when I picture you, what comes to mind is never
Such travellers' constants papering over the gaps,
    But stillness – as if an artist had caught you
    Calmly at ease against

A landscape to which you belong and have belonged always,
Like Mr and Mrs Andrews, on rich home ground –
    Defined not by walls, or even by being
    English or open to the sky,

But simply by being the place where your friends and journeys
Pass through, where you faithfully sow, water the plants
    And share the same love and lightness, always:
    May you not ever move.

THE CEMETERY AT GUFIDAUN

The years flow in and out of the trees,
Neap and summer, winter and spring,
The same slow mulch as the sea.

The starboard lights are steady in the lee
Of the headstones, where the dead are lying
Straight as any tree.

Dressed in their best, they seem to be
In mourning for themselves. You can hear a sighing
Just like the heaving sea.

Over the green waves longingly
Glide their regrets like a great bird flying
Into the rigging of the trees.

Silence, then, or the monody
Of the iron bell in the spire crying
Like a buoy at sea,

Bitter and hard as eternity
Under the cold, bright stars in the sky.
The years flow in and out of the trees,
The same slow mulch as the sea.

FOUR POEMS FOR CHRISTMAS

1

This was the time when ebb and flood
Drowned together, when neap and leaping
Spring, arrested, merged to a sea
Where tufts of spray stood into air
And a calm salt moon basked on slopes
Of solid marble, and in the rigging
Of winter spars the wind steadied
To faithful plainsong.

This was the time when each beacon,
Bright as an icon within its halo,
For one lasting moment, steadily
Gazed and gazed, hope suddenly
No longer occulting. May we too
Rediscover, deeper than dreams
Or tears, the unshifting anchorage of
That shining ocean.

2

On the wind, a drifting echo
of simple songs. In the city
the streetlamps, haloed innocents,
click into instant sleep.
The darkness at last breathes.

In dreams of wholeness, irony
is a train melting to distance;
and the word, a delighted child
gazing in safety at
a star solid as flesh.

3

We bring questionable gifts, the rhetoric
Of pity, to leave here in the brief gap lit
Within the ribs of darkness, the failing flesh
Of God the Word. Here echoes multiply
Of the voice which, out of time, was once to say
Feed my sheep. Now, crib after ragged crib
In the draughty dormitory of hope not quite
Abandoned, spreads its single blanket under
The bleak and beautiful sky. Whose children are these,
The unfed yearlings of Aksum, the ewes of Korem,
The rams of Kobo, the lambs of Alamata?

In a nativity, it is often the baby
You see least. But now come closer, consider
Any of these: look at the brittle pannier
Of bones, the scribbled ribs, the swelling belly
Of emptiness, the cartoon of might have been.
Look at the noble head, too large upon
Its rickety stand, where the flies shift and gleam
In adoring clusters. Approach, as in a dream,
With your small gifts of grain, blankets and bread.
Pray that the manger may yet be filled, the cross
Blossom somehow into a saving star.

4

In the snow-blind blue of winter dark
They re-appear, calm silhouettes
Flattened by familiarity –
Animals, visitors, the holy threesome
Perfectly composed, in the warm light
Gushing earthwards from the chosen star.

Though logic falters, may we still feel
The braille of hope raised – reading this child
As one plucked out of rubble, as the Word
Embossed by love with all the risks
Of blood: and so, even in the cold
Halls of winter, find Christmas real.

AT EASTER

You know, you know
how we never settle,
everywhere darting
like airborne petals.

You know, you know
how we wince and wink,
balancing thinly
on every brink.

You know, you know
how we fall to dust,
a dull powder
fine as rust.

But how Good Friday
becomes the bright O
of the tomb's open door,
do you know? Do you know?

THE LADY CHAPEL, LONG MELFORD

Uncarved by age
the white stones
bandage my eyes:
soft as milk
the walls make
to lap at my soul.

Behind me, death
is a simple door
of gray wood
the worms have made
light as a comb
of drifting sponge.

Nothing here
could be learned or looted:
it is only something
fallen into
from long acceptance,
accrued joy.

Cool as in a dairy
the air hoards
unskimmed light:
without fuss
all the books
have been put aside.

The clock keeps nothing
but nursery time:
each hour
one level chime
taps on the shoulder
and soon is gone.

And from the numbers
set in the wall
the ghosts of children
multiply
their singing way
to white infinity.

The white stones
bandage my eyes:
soft as milk
the walls make
to lap at my soul
with mother-love.

SHRINE

At the crossed feet sprang roses, blood-red
On thorny stems: in the up-ended
Coffin of pain, someone had hooked
A maize cob onto each nailed palm.
Two long, blackening lobes, they looked
Ridiculous, pagan. And twice more
On the same road, this clumsy semaphore
Dangled from the outstretched arms.

Arms still as the trickled blood
That the artist had let dribble from the rood
Down over limbs of painted plaster –
Yet what, in time, most comes across
Is not that god of triumphant disaster
But mortal fruit, the flesh that yields
To time; and over the blackened fields,
The roses' shining gloss.

DETAIL FROM 'ST NICHOLAS REBUKING THE TEMPEST'

A black wind racks the mainsail: stars
Flaring like daisies tell of no good thing.
The whole stout ship is failing – spars
Make signs of the cross. Astern, the ladders trailing
      Are fickle stairs
        Leading to dark despair.

The weather worsens: curling almost
Into a circle, the vessel starts to founder,
The swirling murky waves come coasting
Round the hull like sharks. There are no grounds
      For hope, it seems –
        Until, as in a dream,

At fifty feet above the sea
Saint Nicholas swoops, his hand loaded to bless,
His red chasuble flowing, which must be
Embroidered finely in gold with the letter S:
      Breasting the gale,
        He knows he cannot fail.

A one-man anti-cyclone, he
Will certainly save the day. But why, if so,
Do only some appear to be
Relaxing into faith? What is being thrown
      Over the side
        Into the seething tide?

What is in that parcel, wrapped
In paper and string? What is it in those chests
Heaved onto the gunwhale, strapped
With sturdy rope, that never can be blessed?
      Are they casting out
        The shifting ballast of doubt

Or something truly precious, which slips
Out of reach? You might just note, to the right,
With its sails furled, a tiny ship
Riding quite steadily, safe in the worst of stormlight –
    As if to say
        There might be other ways.

APOLOGIA

Such riddling quiddities, such suppositions!
Men say that Christ at least was in the world,
Even if not of it; while we have turned
Our backs, in order to practise our devotions –
A narrow virtue barely squeezed between
Addiction and indulgence. Do they think
I twitch blindly through from matins and lauds
To compline and the Silence? I know as well
As any man which army's where, or how
To bind a beggar's sores, or what is meant
By swelling in the groin, or gobs of blood.

Lately I did the Psalms – and still like best
The first – the blessing in *Beatus* given
In stem and branch, a pair of crouching lions,
Birds and a cat's mask, the whole most richly done
With vine and oak leaves, brightened with acanthus.
Now, it's the Gospels: on a ground of green,
Light blue and lavender, the drops of gold
Lifted with care across the smooth, ruled vellum.
L for Matthew, already done, then I
For Mark, Q for Luke, then I again
For John – red ivy, with columbine, I think . . .

I do not pretend, as the truly ruthless do,
That any pain can be contracted to fit
The fluency of words or shining paint –
Or that the world's my cloister. All my art,
Beneath rich foliage, curling metaphor,
Commutes between God's world and the trappist heart.
Yet what is learned in silence needs its say –
Next year, if I am spared, I hope to start
On a new challenge, my first Book of Hours.
I shall include St Martin and the Beggar,
And the Virgin helping St Thomas to mend his shirt.

AFTER THE WHALES

Again and again, the suffering of the innocents,
the harpoons blossoming grossly in their bodies:
and when at last the last of the whales is gone,
what will they do, the swarming editors of
the lexicon of greed? Who then will queue
for the flesh rendered to words, the final candles,
corsets, shoe-polish, printer's ink and paint,
gelatine, perfume, pet-food, margarine?
How then will they house the great abstractions,
the faith of sperm whales drifting in calm sleep,
the blue whale's brave loyalty to its love?

Cherish each mortal love, cherish the whale,
lest all those unspoken assumptions by which words live
should be gone with barely a splash, the quick bright flukes
waving farewell again and again, until
we are staring, speechless, at an ocean emptied of song.

OFF WEYMOUTH

Everything perfectly placed – the full quiet moon
Moulding in wax its mussel-shells of light
Over and over the water. Falling astern,
King George's homespun resort shows off its strings
Of bright pearl bulbs. And here, the model steamer
Chugging and chugging, the symmetry of its portholes
Beyond all question, displays a tactful quota
Of passengers on deck, each with a cheek
Angled to catch the best of cool night air.
Full as a frank confession, rounded as truth,
That moon – and that salt air, those riding waves,
The heart almost too full . . . *Yes, I know,
I know. I've seen it too. Let's go below.*

AUDENADE

Departures, season of summaries –
For each anchor weighed,
A cargo of hope to be loaded or discharged:
For each handkerchief waved,
A quickening or tightening of the heart.
The traveller cannot wait to say goodbye,
Cannot bear to gaze any longer at
The brief landscapes of the past, so neatly tied
And bundled out of his path: and yet, as the carriage
Draws away, or the liner slides and slides
Apart from the quay, or the railway carriage clacks
Through the tapping junctions, nor can he bear to say
Farewell, to leave such certainties behind.
Departures, season of summaries and exile –
For each dreamed-of landfall,
A cargo of hope to be salvaged or discharged:
For each handkerchief waved,
A quickening or tightening of the heart.

ROWER

The ocean pushes
off from him:
his blades barely
scuff the trim
nap. Claiming
effort's reward,
he keeps time,
his back to forwards.

Pulling against
strong horizontals
of wind and tide
he feels gerontal:
but goes on ticking
with disciplined pride
to an obbligato
of piratical asides.

Hauling this hull,
he knows, may never
bring him to land
or shift seascapes ever:
but to take the brunt
of neaps and springs
may still define
a kind of living.

THE POET WHO HATED ABROAD

Perhaps he feared the traveller's glib knack
Of conjuring English wheat at either pole,
Of reading any mirage as a varnished boat
Cradled in a lyrical sunset: or could not stomach
Home as an exile's descant, the Sahara sold
For the price of a sob, a fine catch in the throat.

Perhaps he did opt for ease of a kind, by staying
Put, alone, waiting for the one city
To teach him whether the barren might be blessed:
But he also looked unflinchingly, kept on playing
What music he could, assuaged the shades with wit,
Even as door after door drifted onto darkness.

THE ESCAPED NAMES

'He who strives for the escaped names brings to consciousness
others'
Jung

Under the cover of light, the words we choose,
The others have long since gone: and of those that remain,
Which can tell us now their original meanings?
Each venture, it seems, is an old beginning
With equipment so shot and gone that no one would think
Of staging a raid. Or, in another translation,
Lovely enchanting language, sugar-cane,
Honey of roses, whither wilt thou fly?

No end, of course, to our vocabularies,
Evasion after evasion – but who will compile
A dictionary beyond the reach of random,
The impossible esperanto which no one speaks
But all believe in? If we were fluent in that,
Surely those ancestral words would still be waiting
In the echoing belly of the horse, in the old city,
Where now there is only moonlight and scattered stone.

Meanwhile, since there must by definition
Be always at least two ways of looking at things,
Let us, like travellers, be surprised on returning
To find the familiar strange, an otherness even
In our own homes – and be happy to find, at times,
As we look out of the window we thought was a picture,
That a leaf is part of a table; the plain sky,
Simple heaven; a stone, always a stone.

AT WYOMPONT

The path goes up at an angle,
Through mid-spectral evergreens,
Past tangles of barbed briars
And the sun's searchlight sweeping
The dangerous clearings. Birdsong
Is a sly enticement to shadow.
Here the pursued are always
Too slow: and even in mist
You see the lolling pink tongues
Of the dogs, and the broad legs
Of the high wooden towers.

One scraggy hilltop oak
Remembers resistance – the six
Last months of life for three.
Six months of berries bleeding
In their mouths, and the dry acoustic
Of fear, before they were found
And shot, a year too soon.
Three small crosses, and one
Oval photograph weeping
In its frame: *notre cher fils*.
A few plastic flowers.

What use, what possible use?
The wrong question nags
With more than simple hindsight –
For somewhere, even now,
A hooped lorry is lurching
Empty, back along
A forest track, from
Freshly turned earth:
And in other forests, primed
Khaki or silver pens
Are waiting to write *The End*.

Below the woods, close
To the old Roman bridge
At Wyompont, pink blossom
Is flaking once again
Into the swift small stream,
To be whirled away. Always
Tyranny – always this sad
Shedding of blossom and blood,
So that deciduous hope
In honour of those who resist
May continue to bear fruit.

THE DART ESTUARY: WHITSUNDAY

What light could be more generous than this?
A million multiples of here and now
Tingle on the face of the water, kiss after kiss.

For hours, from high on a hill, came the crackling morse
Of guns, where tiny marksmen lobbed clay disks
Up into blue, by a vivid crescent of gorse.

Lower, a steam train passed, squirting smoke in plumes
Out through steep trees. To the west, a naval band
Wrestled with a tune that wobbled in the wind's volume.

Now, near evening, the lavish boats
Nod to the last of themselves. Along the shore,
In oil-green shadows, a hazy stillness floats.

The silence hums, a treasure-house of each
Glint of sound, where all the colours melt
To gold and then to blankness, uncoined speech.

Mast-high already, springing clear above,
The wafery moon swells to its own calm gloss,
Subsuming every language under love.

THE ARTIST AT 81

Plain truth has become his only ornament,
Beguilement, first nature. With one white handkerchief
He will conjure the real world! Each hydra hand
Will meet the span required.

His repertoire goes down like a favourite meal:
His mind and heart savour the exact weight
Of all the notes as, one by one, they ripen
Each in its own tempo.

It does not surprise him that the audience weeps:
Long ago, tears were the motherland
Of all his craft, twins to the blinding gems
Pinned to a tyrant's chest.

In this, his fine economy of age,
Nothing is show. Simply his music spells
A fluency of blessing to drown out
The worst of history. He need not even look
To know that we are weeping.